FESTIVAL OF FAITH

A Cantata by Joseph M. Martin

Orchestrations by Brant Adams and Stan Pethel

① This symbol indicates a track number on the StudioTrax CD or SplitTrax CD.

Duration: ca. 46 Minutes

ISBN 9-781-5400-3653-7

SHAWNEE PRESS

EXCLUSIVELY DISTRIBUTED BY

HAL•LEONARD®

7777 W. BLUEMOUND RD. P.O. BOX 13819 MILWAUKEE, WI 53213

Visit Hal Leonard Online at
www.halleonard.com

Visit Shawnee Press Online at
www.shawneepress.com

Contact us:
Hal Leonard
7777 West Bluemound Road
Milwaukee, WI 53213
Email: info@halleonard.com

In Europe, contact:
Hal Leonard Europe Limited
Distribution Centre, Newmarket Road
Bury St Edmunds, Suffolk, IP33 3YB
Email: info@halleonardeurope.com

In Australia, contact:
Hal Leonard Australia Pty. Ltd.
4 Lentara Court
Cheltenham, Victoria, 3192 Australia
Email: info@halleonard.com.au

FOREWORD

We are a people of the Song.

From generation to generation, worshippers have shared their spiritual journeys through the sacred arts. Our tuneful testimonies are passionate witnesses to the miracles God has worked among His people. Hymns, psalms and spiritual songs provide the church with a special language of the heart as we share and remember our heritage of faith.

With music we comfort each other during difficult times, singing promises of hope and peace. The great hymns and treasured psalms enrich and encourage us by pressing God's timeless truths deep into our yearning hearts and minds. When we sing, we breathe together and, in that unity, we celebrate our calling as people of praise. It is in these precious, holy moments that our grateful voices of worship rise like incense to the Giver of grace. In the hushed spaces between the words and notes, we listen and learn.

So now as we gather to hear these timeless truths, once again we experience the mystery and majesty of Christ's redemptive love. May each song remind us to celebrate life and inspire our living to become a joyful festival of faith.

PERFORMANCE NOTES

"FESTIVAL OF FAITH" is a celebration of life based on the ministry, passion and resurrection of Jesus. The work is designed to share the timeless message of hope and grace through treasured hymns and classic lyrics. Mingling time-honored tunes and texts with more recently composed music provides a balance of the familiar with the new. The scripture-based narration gives the piece an almost "Lessons and Carols" spirit and is crafted to work using either a single reader or multiple readers. Feel free to adapt the presentation by including drama, liturgical movement or sacred symbols to enhance your congregation's worship experience. The last two movements of the work are post-Easter and may be performed separately for those churches wishing to present this cantata during Holy Week.

PROCESSION OF FAITH

Tune: **PALAD...**
Music...
JOSEPH M. MARTIN (B...

27 **With power and majesty** (♩= ca. 69)

AND CAN IT BE THAT I SHOULD GAIN

Words by
CHARLES WESLEY (1707-1788)

Tune: SAGI...
by THOMAS CAMPBELL (1777-18...
Arranged...
JOSEPH M. MARTIN (B...

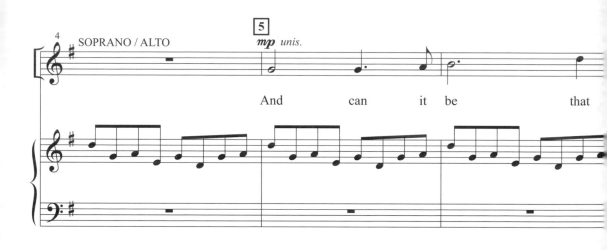

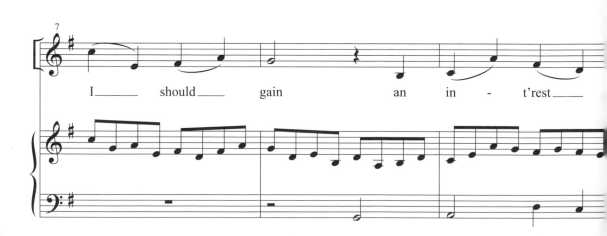

in my _____ Sav - ior's blood?

TENOR / BASS
mp *unis.*

Died He for me, who _____ caused His

mf

mp

be that Thou,____ my____ God,____ should____

die for____ me!

He left His

(opt. a cappell
through m. 52.

Fa - ther's throne _____ a - bove, _____ so
free, ___ so ___ in - fi - nite His ___ grace. _____
Emp - tied Him - self _____ of all but

love, and bled____ for Ad - am's

help - less race. 'Tis mer - cy

all, im - mense____ and____ free;____ for,

A - live in Him,____ my liv - ing Head,____ and clothed____ in right - eous - ness di - vine,

maz - ing love! A - maz - ing

grace! A - maz - ing love of

God! _____

NARRATOR:

The beginning of the good news about Jesus the Messiah, the Son of God, as it is written in Isaiah the prophet:

"I will send My messenger ahead of You,
who will prepare Your way;
a voice of one calling in the wilderness,
Prepare the way for the Lord,
make straight the path before Him."

And so John the Baptist appeared in the wilderness, preaching a baptism of repentance for the forgiveness of sins. The whole Judean countryside and all the people of Jerusalem went out to him. And this was his message:

"After me comes one more powerful than I. I baptize you with water,
but He will baptize you with the Holy Spirit."

(Mark 1:1-8 paraphrased)

A CALL TO FAITH

Words and Music by
JOSEPH M. MARTIN (BMI)
Incorporating Tune:
NEUMARK
by GEORG NEUMARK (1621-1681)

Lyrics: This is a time for signs and

There is a new song in the light.

O - pen your hearts; pre - pare, pre - pare.

Long we have

hope___ for ju-bi - lee. There is a new song in the air. O - pen your hearts; pre - pare, pre - pare.

This is the mo - ment. This is the place!

O - pen your life to God's mir - a - cle ways!_____

This is the mo - ment. This is the place!

Come, know the won - der of grace. Come, know the

won - der of grace.

Lord, we have wept a thou - sand riv - ers, bend - ing our

knees on for-eign sands; pray-ing that

You will soon de - liv - er, bring-ing us

to our prom - ised land! There is a

NARRATOR:

After John was put in prison, Jesus went all over Galilee, proclaiming the good news of God. He taught in the places of worship, and healed all kinds of sickness and disease among the people. Jesus saw many seekers and when He went up a mountain and sat down, His followers came to Him, and He began to teach.

(Mark 1:14 paraphrased)

COME TO THE MOUNTAIN

Words and Music by
JOSEPH M. MARTIN (BMI)

FESTIVAL OF FAITH - SATB

TENOR / BASS
mf unis.

Come to the moun - tain, Je - sus is preach - ing;

shar - ing the gos - pel of love___ and peace,

shar - ing the gos - pel of peace.

mp

Come to the lake-side, Jesus is heal-ing. Come, touch the teach-er of Gal-i-lee.

Oo

Come, touch the teach-er of Gal - i-lee. Come to the lake-side, truth is re-veal-ing;

won - ders of mer - cy so rich____ and free,

mer - cy so rich____ and free.

Come, come to the moun - tain. Come, rest in the

Lord. Come, seek - ers of grace. Come to the

place where hope is re - stored!_____ Come to where hope is re -

stored!

Come to the jour - ney, Je - sus is call - ing,

"Take up your cross___ and fol - low Me." Come to the jour - ney,

walk in His foot-steps; trust in the Shep-herd wher -

ev - er He leads. Trust Him wher - ev - er He

leads._____ Trust in the Lord. O

Trust in the Lord. Trust Him wher-ev-er He

NARRATOR:

And great multitudes came to Jesus, bringing with them those who were lame, crippled, blind, and mute, and many others; and He healed them. The crowd marveled at what they saw, and they glorified God for such great miracles.

(Matthew 15:30 paraphrased)

PRAYER OF RESTORATION

Words by
CLARA H. SCOTT (1841-1897), alt
Additional Words: JOSEPH M. MARTIN

Music
SARA R. NUSSEL (ASCA

Arranged
JOSEPH M. MARTIN (BM

me. Place in my hands＿＿＿ the won-drous key. Let it un-

lock＿＿＿＿＿ and＿ set me free.

(end solo or section)

T. *mp* unis.

B.

O - pen my

S. *mp* unis.

A.

O - pen my ears, that I may hear

ears,＿＿＿＿＿ that＿ I may hear the voice of

the voice of truth   You're send-ing clear, and while the

truth_____ You're_ send - ing   clear,

sounds_____ fall   on   my   ear,   then   all things

false_____ will dis-ap-pear._____   O - pen my ears, and_ let m

see. O - pen my life, il - lu - mine me.

O - pen my mouth,_____ and__ let me sing.

O - pen my mouth,

Lord, take my song_____ in__ of - fer

and let me sing. Lord, take my song in

ing. O - pen my mind, o - pen my

of - fer - ing.

heart, re - store my joy, let heal-ing start.

Re-store my joy, let healing start. O - pen my

NARRATOR:

When Jesus and His disciples had come near Jerusalem and reached the Mount of Olives, Jesus sent two disciples, saying,

> "Go into the village ahead of you, and immediately you will find a donkey tied, and a colt with her. Untie them and bring them to Me."

The disciples went and did as Jesus had directed them. They brought the donkey and the colt, and put their cloaks on them and He sat on them. A very large crowd spread their cloaks on the road, and others cut branches from the trees and spread them on the ground before Him. The crowd that went ahead of Him, and that followed, were shouting,

> "Hosanna to the Son of David!
> Blessed is the one who comes in the name of the Lord!
> Hosanna in the highest heaven!"

(Matthew 21:1-2, 6-9 NRSV*)

FESTIVAL OF PALMS

Words by
JOSEPH M. MARTIN (BMI)

Based on tu
LASST UNS ERFREU
Geistliche Kirchengesäng, 1
Arranged
JOSEPH M. MART

down your gar-ments; clear the way! _____ Sing ho-san - na! Sing ho san - na! Sing ho-san - na! Sing ho-san - na! Sing ho-

san - na to the King of kings!

ring! Each voice raised in grate - ful of - fer

ing. Sing ho - san - na! Sing ho - san - na! Sing h

san - na! Sing ho - san - na! Sing ho - san - na to the King of

kings!

san - na! Come, ___ long - a - wait - ed Prince of

Peace! ___ Make ev - 'ry war and con - flict cease! ___

Sing ho

Sing ho - san - na! Sing ho - san - na! Sing ho

san - na!

NARRATOR:

Then came the day of Unleavened Bread on which the Passover lamb had to be sacrificed. Jesus sent Peter and John, saying,

> "Go and make preparation for us to eat the Passover."

When the hour came, Jesus and His apostles reclined at the table, and He said to them,

> "I have eagerly desired to eat this Passover with you before I suffer."

And He took bread, gave thanks and broke it, and gave it to them saying,

> "This is My body given for you; do this in remembrance of Me."

In the same way, after the supper He took the cup saying,

> "This cup is the new covenant in My blood, which is poured out for you."

(Luke 22:7-8, 14-20 paraphrased)

IN THE BREAKING OF THE BREAD

Words and Music
JOSEPH M. MARTIN (BM

ta - ble of the Lord, our hearts are fed. There is

grace in the break - ing of the bread. In___ the

TENOR / BASS

In the pour - ing of the wine, in the

lift - ing, in___ the bless - ing, we___ are

lift - ing of the cup, in the bless - ing of the vine, we are

filled with heav-en's love. At the ta-ble of the Lord, we see the

sign. There is grace in the pour-ing of the wine. There is

par - don. There is mer - cy. There is heal-ing. There is

wor-ship, in the praise, in our ser-vice, in our prayer, in the
mu-sic that we raise, in the fel-low-ship we share, at the
ta-ble of the Lord, we find our place.

In the

NARRATOR:

Then Jesus went with His disciples to a place called Gethsemane, and He said to them,

> "Sit here while I go over there and pray. My soul is overwhelmed with sorrow to the point of death. Stay here and watch with Me."

Going a little further, He fell, with His face to the ground, and fervently prayed,

> "My Father, if it is possible, may this cup be taken from Me.
> Yet not as I will, but let Your will be done."

(Mark 14:32-36 paraphrased)

SHADOW GARDEN

Words and Music by
JOSEPH M. MARTIN (BMI)

With ev-'ry breath of wind,___ the gar-den moves in whis-pered sighs.

Oo___

7
unis.
Dark Ju - de - an
A sil - ver moon is ris - ing in - to the dark Ju - de - an
7
9
mf
skies.
mf
skies.
9
mf
11
mp
Shad-ows from o - live trees touch Je - sus as He grieves,
mp
11
mp

pour - ing out His heart in ag - on - y.

The drone of dis - tant thun - der

ech - oes through-out the sol - emn night.

70

know-ing His time is near. Hear Him groan in an-guish and in

fear. _____ Come ___ to the gar - den.

Fall on your knees. _____ Kneel in the

shad - ows, the shad - ows of Geth - sem - a -

ne.

cresc. poco a poco

con forza

And now come cries of vio - lence. With torch - es high, the sol - diers

march.

One kiss be - trays the Sa - cred be - neath the gar - den's an - cient

"Fa - ther, Fa - ther,

let Thy will be done in Me!

Fa - ther, Fa - ther,

76

let Thy will be done_____ in

Me!

Thy will be done!"_____

FESTIVAL OF FAITH - SA

NARRATOR:

So, Jesus was arrested, tried under Pontius Pilate, and sentenced to die by crucifixion. Carrying His own cross, He was taken out to the place of the skull, which is called Golgotha. There they crucified Him, and with Him two others…one on each side and Jesus in the middle. Pilate had a notice prepared and fastened to the cross. It read,

"Jesus of Nazareth, the King of the Jews."

(John 19:16-20 paraphrased)

I SAW THE CROSS OF JESUS

Words by
FREDERICK WHITFIELD (1829-1904), alt.
With Additional Words by
JOSEPH M. MARTIN (BMI)

Music
JOSEPH M. MART

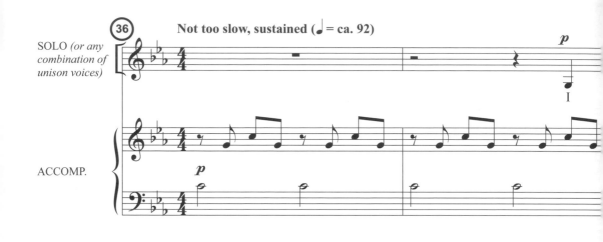

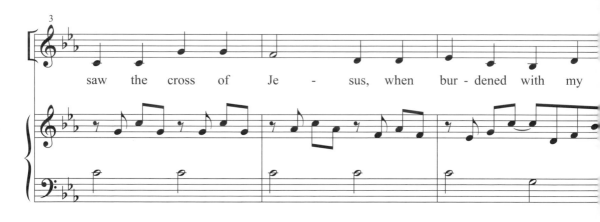

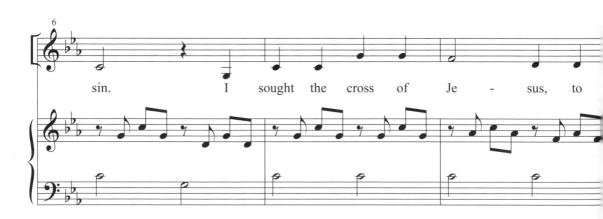

give me peace with - in. I

brought my soul to Je - sus. He cleansed it in His

blood; and in the cross of Je - sus,____

____ I____ found my peace with God.

His— tears of grace re - store.

Sure - ly, sure - ly,

Christ has known our mourn - ing.——

and with His wounds, our bro-ken lives are healed.

grace has made me whole.

One

day in strains of glo - ry, I'll sing on heav - en's

shore, where sin can nev - er en - ter in, ____

____ and ____ death is known no more, and ____

death is known no more, no

no more.

NARRATOR:
(This narration may be read during the introduction to "EASTER PEOPLE, RISE" (page 91, measures 1-19)).

After the Sabbath, at the dawn of the first day of the week, Mary Magdalene and the other Mary went to look at the tomb.

There was a violent earthquake, for an angel of the Lord came down from heaven, and, going to the tomb, rolled back the stone and sat upon it. The angel's appearance was like lightning, and his robes were white as snow.

The angel said to the women,

> "Do not be afraid, for I know that you are looking for Jesus, who was crucified. He is not here. He has risen, just as He said. Go quickly, and tell His disciples that Jesus has risen from the dead."

Alleluia! Christ is risen indeed!

(Matthew 28:1-6 paraphrased)

EASTER PEOPLE, RISE

Tune: **PALADIN**
Words and Music by
JOSEPH M. MARTIN (BMI)

* Part for congregation is on page 109.

SOPRANO / ALTO
(opt. unison on melody)

Eas - ter peo - ple, lift your heads.

Je - sus is no long - er dead.___ See the gar - den

now re - stored. Praise to our ma - jes - tic Lord!

With majesty (♩ = ca. 80)
SOPRANO DESCANT

Eas-ter peo - ple, raise your_ voice! With cre - a - tion,_

Eas - ter peo-ple,_ raise your voice!_ With cre - a - tion,_

With majesty (♩ = ca. 80)

now re - joice!____ Death has dropped its sword of doom.

now re - joice!____ Death__ has__ dropped its sword__ of doom.

Mu - sic pours__ from__ ev - 'ry tomb.____ Mu - sic pours__ from

Mu - sic pours from ev - 'ry tomb. Mu - sic pours from

commissioned by the Chancel Choir, staff, and congregation of Fallston United Methodist Church, Fallston, Maryland,
in honor of Frederick Rheinhardt on the occasion of his 60 years as church musician, 1955-2015

A CALL TO ALLELUIA

Words and Music
JOSEPH M. MARTIN (BM
Incorporating tur
ENGELBER
by CHARLES V. STANFORD (1852-192

joy - ful noise. Let ev - 'ry na - tion raise a

no - ble voice. In cel - e - bra - tion, let the

church re - joice. Al - le - lu - ia!

cresc. poco a poco

cresc. poco a poco

cresc. poco a poco

lu - ia! Al - le - lu - ia!

Now let your voic - es be an in - stru-ment of

104

Let_ true_ ad - o - ra - tion start.

song and_ let_ true_ ad - o - ra - tion start.

With mer - cy, love and grace, live out your

songs of praise. Serve God with glad - ness all your

days.

Set free a song of joy____ in ev-'ry place.____

Re-deem the wrong and raise____ a hymn of grace.____

Let hearts be strong and tuned for love and joy - ful praise!

Al - le - lu - ia! Al - le -

lu - ia! Al - le - lu - ia! Al - le - lu - ia!

Sing al - le - lu - ia!

The publisher hereby grants permission to reprint the material within the box for the purpose of making performance of this cantata possible with congregational participation, provided that a sufficient quantity of copies of the entire cantata has been purchased for performance by the choir and accompanist. The music must be reproduced with the title and all credits including the copyright notice.

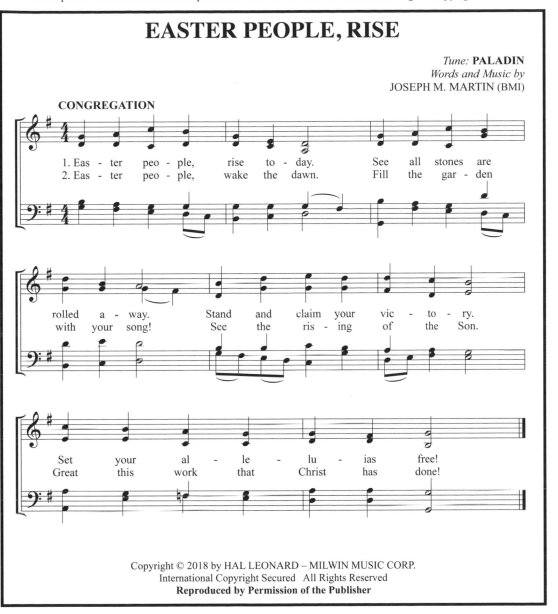

EASTER PEOPLE, RISE

Tune: **PALADIN**
Words and Music by
JOSEPH M. MARTIN (BMI)

CONGREGATION

1. Eas - ter peo - ple, rise to - day. See all stones are rolled a - way. Stand and claim your vic - to - ry. Set your al - le - lu - ias free!
2. Eas - ter peo - ple, wake the dawn. Fill the gar - den with your song! See the ris - ing of the Son. Great this work that Christ has done!